THE DEFINITIVE COLORADO BUCKET LIST

GUIDE BOOK

Over 110 Captivating Destinations and Discovery Nooks to Transform Your Travel Wishes into Everlasting Memories! + Colorado Map & Journal Log Section

Sam Miller

Credits

1. File Source: https://unsplash.com/it/foto/un-fiume-che-attraversa-un-canyon-circondato-da-montagne-45ghEvyBya8
License Details: https://unsplash.com/it/plus/licenza
Author: Unsplash+ in collaboration with Getty Images
2. File Source: https://unsplash.com/it/foto/una-staccionata-di-legno-con-vista-sulle-montagne-sullo-sfondo-M8OHP76krDM
License Details: https://unsplash.com/it/plus/licenza
Author: Unsplash+ in collaboration with Josh Hild
3. File Source: https://gisgeography.com/colorado-map/
License Details: Free License for Educational and Commercial Uses
Source: GISGeography.com
4. File Source: https://gisgeography.com/colorado-map/
License Details: Free License for Educational and Commercial Uses
Source: GISGeography.com
5. File Source: https://unsplash.com/it/foto/una-veduta-aerea-di-un-canyon-con-una-montagna-sullo-sfondo-PCclZvQ1_Rs
License Details: https://unsplash.com/it/plus/licenza
Author: Unsplash+ in collaboration with Getty Images
6. File Source: https://unsplash.com/it/foto/livros-e-lapis-no-mapa-Af8ZjGMsHKQ
License Details: https://unsplash.com/it/licenza
Author: Picture by John Matychuk on Unsplash
7. File Source: https://commons.wikimedia.org/wiki/File:Maroon_Bells_(11553)a.jpg
License Details: https://creativecommons.org/licenses/by-sa/4.0/deed.en
Author: Picture by Rhododendrites

8. File Source:
    https://commons.wikimedia.org/wiki/File:Eldorado_Canyon_Sta
    te_Park.JPG
    License Details: https://creativecommons.org/licenses/by-
    sa/3.0/deed.en
    Author: Picture by Jeffrey Beall from Wikimedia Commons
9. File Source:
    https://commons.wikimedia.org/wiki/File:Garden_of_the_Gods_
    central_gardens_from_the_north.jpg
    License Details: https://creativecommons.org/licenses/by-
    sa/4.0/deed.en
    Author: Picture of Dicklyon
10. File Source:
    https://www.flickr.com/photos/daveynin/9591502923/
    License Details:
    https://creativecommons.org/licenses/by/4.0/deed.en
    Author: Picture of Visitor7 from Wikimedia Commons
11. File Source:
    https://commons.wikimedia.org/wiki/File:Moraine_Park_Valley,
    _Rocky_Mountain_National_Park.jpg
    License Details: https://creativecommons.org/licenses/by-
    sa/4.0/deed.en
    Author: Picture of Frank Schulenburg
12. File Source:
    https://commons.wikimedia.org/wiki/File:Colorado_National_M
    onument_(35c59f40-a020-4bc5-9c99-e042fc6f2f86).jpg
    License Details: Public Domain
    Author: Source: NPGallery, Photographer: Victoria Stauffenberg
13. File Source:
    https://commons.wikimedia.org/wiki/File:Million_Dollar_Highw
    ay_09_2006_09_13.jpg
    License Details: https://creativecommons.org/licenses/by-
    sa/3.0/deed.en

Author: Picture of Andreas F. Borchert from Wikimedia Commons

14. File Source: https://unsplash.com/it/foto/vista-dallalto-di-una-giovane-coppia-irriconoscibile-con-mappe-che-pianificano-il-viaggio-di-vacanza-concetto-di-viaggio-desktop-lSJebMiPMk0
    License Details: https://unsplash.com/it/plus/licenza
    Author: Unsplash+ in collaboration with Getty Images

15. Cover Image: https://www.shutterstock.com/it/image-photo/mountain-valley-rocky-mountains-canada-picturesque-1413292532
    License Details: Roaylty-free
    Cover Elements File Source: https://it.freepik.com/vettori-gratuito/set-di-cornici-per-foto_5358545.htm#query=pin%20polaroid&position=0&from_view=search&track=ais

16. License type: Free License/Public Domain
    Author: Image by pch.vector on Freepik

17. Cover Elements File Source: https://www.freepik.com/free-vector/usa-license-plate-set_8610451.htm#query=usa%20license%20plate&position=12&from_view=keyword&track=ais
    License type: Free License/Public Domain
    Author: Image by macrovector_official on Freepik

4

Legal & Disclaimer © 2023

before using any of the suggested remedies, techniques, or information in this book.

(1)

Table of Contents

About Colorado

(2)

Adventuring through new places often brings a mix of excitement and apprehension. You're seeking more than just stunning scenery. What you really want is to grasp the essence and local flavor that turns an ordinary vacation into a profoundly rewarding experience. While the internet may provide an alluring preview, it frequently fails to capture the local rhythm that pulses in sync with an area. For that reason, you need a guide that goes above and beyond the norm and dives into the mystique of Colorado.

This guide is your personal assistant for unveiling the spectacular beauty and lively spirit of Colorado. It is created by blending local expertise with a deep appreciation for the diverse terrain. This pocket guide will lead you to uncover hidden gems along with Colorado's most acclaimed marvels. The book is a treasure chest crafted from local tales, brimming with insights only a knowledgeable Colorado resident can provide.

The authenticity is founded on an intimate understanding of Colorado's landscapes and customs, as well as the endless adventures that beckon. It's more than just an itinerary. It's an entry point to a world where every path tells a story, each town has a legend, and every dawn is a stunning palette of hues adorning the skies above the Rockies.

Having this guide at your side offers many benefits. It's your route to the energetic city of Denver and your guide to the peaceful trails of Aspen, as well as your companion amid the ancient echoes of Mesa Verde. It's the insider whisperings and wisdom embedded in every recommendation, the stories that bring each location to life.

To provide a glimpse of the riches to come, did you know there is an extensive network of mysterious underground tunnels existing below the modern commotion of the city? Or that the charming town of Telluride was once home to Butch Cassidy? These tales, paired with valuable tips and charming whispers, make this book a treasure.

This guide promises a journey filled with discoveries, sprinkled with laughter, and colored by the vibrant hues of Colorado's breathtaking landscapes. It is your ticket to a road less traveled, a more intimate and completely captivating Colorado.

However, remember that the allure of Colorado is as boundless as the vast horizon, unveiling new stories, sights, and trails each day. Thus, the essence of today beckons you, and tomorrow may reveal a brand new adventure.

The Map of Colorado

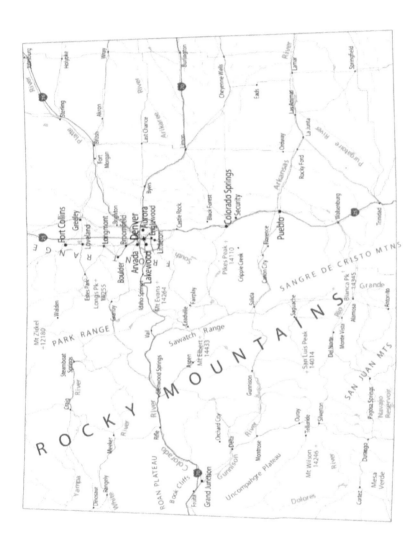

(3)

(Cities and Roads)

(4)

(Parks and Lakes)

Why Visit Colorado?

(5)

Colorado is a vast expanse of varied landscapes, acting as a magnet for the curious, brave, and those captivated by the astounding. Its appeal goes far beyond the sweeping vistas, tucked away in the myriad adventures winding through icy peaks, charming villages, vibrant cities, and peaceful wooded trails.

A distinctive draw of Colorado is its changing seasons, each unveiling uniquely sublime experiences. Winter ushers in a warm welcome to the slopes, where skiers can indulge in America's premier skiing and snowboarding destinations. Locales like Aspen, Vail, and Breckenridge pulsate with energy when blankets of snow transform the terrain into a winter wonderland, adorned with every snowflake in Colorado's enchanting seasonal tale.

As the snow melts away, paths meander through alpine meadows, across rugged topography, finally immersing you in Colorado's untamed heart.

Cyclists, hikers, and nature enthusiasts find refuge in the warm hues of a Colorado spring and summer. Towns like Boulder, Colorado Springs, and Estes Park morph into gateways to countless trails, each presenting a chance to revel in nature's breathtaking splendor.

Additionally, Colorado's rich history adds a compelling new dimension. Ancient cliff dwellings in Mesa Verde recount tales of bygone civilizations, while the Victorian charm of Georgetown juxtaposed with Denver's contemporary excitement offers a glimpse into Colorado's evolving narrative.

The cultural heartbeat, embodied in festivals like the Telluride Film Festival, infuses Colorado's towns with an amalgam of international and local flavors. This mosaic extends to the culinary scene, where farm-to-table eateries and upstart breweries highlight Colorado's bountiful harvest.

It's also impossible to overlook the tranquility of Colorado's many rivers and lakes, whose calm waters mirror the sky and soothe the soul, beckoning anglers.

Colorado is more than a casual destination; it's a trove of experiences waiting to be unearthed. It's where the thrill of adventure intertwines with nature's tranquility, an oasis for adrenaline junkies and peace-seekers alike. It's where history's whispers converge with modern-day zeal, fostering appreciation for this magnificent land.

In the forthcoming chapters, you'll delve into what makes Colorado so alluring. The diverse landscapes, each with their own charm and tale, tempt you with the promise of exploration awaiting your footsteps along the roads that compose Colorado, the Centennial State.

How to Use the Book

(6)

This guidebook is designed for effortless trip planning, with a wealth of information at your fingertips. Let's explore the user-friendly layout crafted to enrich your Colorado adventure.

Maps: You'll find a comprehensive Colorado maps destined to become your exploration mate. It's more than pins and lines—it's your route to where Colorado's treasures lie. If a highlighted locale entices you, the maps reveal its location within Colorado's expansive terrain.

City-Based Organization: The guide's content is structured city-by-city, charting a clear course through the many experiences each urban hub and surrounding area offers. Under each city's banner is an array of spots with unique appeal and amenities. This system lets you go in-depth in one city or hop between locations, customizing your journey.

Detailed Listings: Here's what you'll find in each place entry:

Why Visit: A brief excerpt explaining its allure and why it should top your Colorado wishlist.

Best Time to Visit: Recommendations on optimal dates considering weather and events, so you can capture its essence.

Location: A geographical overview for context.

Directions: Simple directions from the nearest town or landmark to get you there.

GPS Coordinates: Ensuring you're on track.

Nearest Town: Serving as a reference point and potential starting point to explore from.

Interesting Facts: Sparking curiosity with fascinating historical tidbits.

The goal is providing the essential details in an engaging manner, crafting a seamless travel experience. Each section artfully blends vital information, compelling stories, and practical tips to enrich your adventures through Colorado's stunning landscapes.

ASPEN

Maroon Bells

(7)

Why You Should Visit: The captivating Maroon Bells are considered one of America's most photographed vistas, boasting stunning twin peaks ensconced within a glacial valley. This natural beauty epitomizes the treasures Aspen proudly displays.

Best Time to Visit: Mid-June through early October.

Location: Just 10 miles west of Aspen, Colorado.

Directions: From Aspen, follow Maroon Creek Road straight to the Bells. A shuttle from Aspen Highlands Ski Area provides access during summer and fall.

GPS Coordinates: 39.0703° N, 106.9878° W

Nearest Town: Aspen

Interesting Facts: The bells get their name from the uniquely shaped, maroon-hued mountains. This striking color comes from mudstone reflecting light to radiate a maroon shimmer.

Ashcroft Ghost Town

Why You Should Visit: Step back in time at Ashcroft Ghost Town, a portal into Colorado's rich mining history. The well-preserved ghost town transports visitors to the late 19th century, unveiling the remains of a once-thriving mining community. It's an intriguing journey into the past.

Best Time to Visit: Late summer or early fall allows you to explore without icy routes.

Location: Nestled 11 miles south of Aspen, Colorado.

Directions: Head south on Castle Creek Road from Aspen. The 25-minute drive leads to this abandoned relic.

GPS Coordinates: 39.0194° N, 106.8200° W

Nearest Town: Aspen

Interesting Facts: During its heyday, over 3,500 people inhabited Ashcroft's bustling streets. It was poised to boom into a major mining hub but was soon eclipsed by nearby Aspen's growing affluence.

Independence Ghost Town

Why You Should Visit: Independence Ghost Town unveils another integral chapter in Colorado's enduring mining history. The well-preserved relics quietly recount tales of mining pioneers facing hardship and hope, set against a naturally picturesque backdrop perfect for photography and history buffs.

Best Time to Visit: Enjoy summer's warmth when trails are accessible and the park is inviting.

Location: 35241-, 36221 CO-82, Aspen.

Directions: An easy drive down Highway 82 from Aspen leads to this charming historic retreat.

GPS Coordinates: 39.1081° N, 106.5649° W

Nearest Town: Aspen

Interesting Facts: Founded in 1879, Independence was one of the first Roaring Fork Valley settlements. It was named in honor of its patron saint, the 4th of July, commemorating the town's birthdate.

John Denver Sanctuary

Why You Should Visit: The John Denver Sanctuary is a peaceful tribute to the beloved singer-songwriter, whose musical legacy was entwined with his passion for nature and Colorado. More than honoring Denver's enduring impact, it's a tranquil spot to unwind, with rock terraces and lyrical extracts set along the calming Roaring Fork River. The ideal place for reflection and relaxation.

Best Time to Visit: Late spring through early summer.

Location: 470 Rio Grande Pl, Aspen.

Directions: From downtown Aspen, head to Rio Grande Place. A short walk leads you to the sanctuary.

GPS Coordinates: 39.1867° N, 106.8186° W

Nearest Town: Aspen

Interesting Facts: The sanctuary also hosts community gatherings and is home to Aspen's largest perennial garden.

Silver Queen Gondola

Why You Should Visit: Soar up the slopes of Aspen Mountain on the scenic Silver Queen Gondola, treating your eyes to jaw-dropping panoramic views of the surrounding snow-capped peaks and lush green valleys. A skier's paradise transforms into a mountain biking and hiking haven come summer.

Best Time to Visit: Ski in winter or hike and bike in summer.

Location: 611 E Durant Ave, Aspen.

Directions: The gondola station is located downtown. Just follow signs to the station.

GPS Coordinates: 39.1868° N, 106.8186° W

Nearest Town: Aspen

Interesting Facts: The 14-minute ride to the summit gives you ample time to soak in the breathtaking vistas.

Independence Pass

Why You Should Visit: Feel your heart race as you ascend to exhilarating heights on Independence Pass, which features an adrenaline-pumping drive dotted with places to stop and be awe-inspired by the majestic Rocky Mountain views all around. It's also a gateway to outdoor adventures, with abundant biking and hiking trails to satisfy your thirst for an active alpine escape.

Best Time to Visit: Late spring through early autumn.

Location: East of Aspen along Highway 82.

Directions: From Aspen, head east on E Cooper Ave, then continue on CO-82 E to reach this breathtaking spot.

GPS Coordinates: 39.1083° N, 106.5639° W

Nearest Town: Aspen

Interesting Facts: Cresting at 12,095 feet, it holds the distinction as one of Colorado's highest paved mountain passes.

AURORA

Cherry Creek State Park

Why You Should Visit: Cherry Creek State Park unveils an outdoor enthusiast's paradise, nature's playground inviting leisurely strolls. The sprawling reservoir provides ideal jet skiing, boating, and fishing, while the landscape lends itself to cycling, hiking, birdwatching, and biking.

Best Time to Visit: May-August for water activities. March-May or September-November for hiking and birding.

Location: 4201 S Parker Rd, Aurora, CO.

Directions: From Aurora, head south on S Abilene St, turn right on E Parker Rd, and continue straight until Cherry Creek State Park is on your left.

GPS Coordinates: 39.6403° N, 104.8474° W

Nearest Town: Aurora

Interesting Facts: A wildlife refuge for graceful deer, elusive coyotes, and over 40 bird species, making it a photographer's delight.

Aurora Reservoir

Why You Should Visit: The peaceful and inviting Aurora Reservoir is a wonderful spot to relax on the sandy banks, cast your line for trout, or float serenely across the calm waters on a boat or stand-up paddleboard. It also features an 8-mile multi-use trail perfect for cycling, running, or taking a leisurely stroll along the shoreline.

Best Time to Visit: May-August for boating and beach fun. Fish year-round.

Location: 5800 S Powhaton Rd, Aurora, CO.

Directions: From Aurora, take E Quincy Ave and S Gun Club Rd to E Jewell Ave. Follow E Jewell Ave and S Powhaton Rd to reach the reservoir.

GPS Coordinates: 39.6289° N, 104.7059° W

Nearest Town: Aurora

Interesting Facts: A community hub offering seasonal events like fishing tournaments and lively summer concerts.

Plains Conservation Center

Why You Should Visit: The Plains Conservation Center provides a wonderful opportunity to immerse yourself in Colorado's vast prairie ecosystem, discover intriguing details about the area's rich history, and maybe even spot some incredible resident wildlife in their natural habitat. This fascinating excursion is laced with adventure for nature lovers.

Best Time to Visit: March-May and September-November offer mild weather and glimpses of native flora.

Location: 21901 E Hampden Ave, Aurora, CO.

Directions: From E 6th Ave, take the E470 N exit and follow E470 N to E Hampden Ave.

GPS Coordinates: 39.6536° N, 104.7475° W

Nearest Town: Aurora

Interesting Facts: Features replica sod houses and teepees providing insights into prairie pioneers' and Native Americans' daily life.

Aurora History Museum

Why You Should Visit: As a community-centered hub, the Aurora History Museum is the ideal place to take a fascinating look back through time as you explore the city's evolution and development over the decades. Rotating exhibits shine a spotlight on various aspects of local history, culture, nature, and art.

Best Time to Visit: Year-round, especially during Aurora's lively event seasons like fall.

Location: 15051 E Alameda Pkwy, Aurora, CO

Directions: From I-225 take exit 7 to E Mississippi Ave, head west, turn right on S Sable Blvd, left on E Alameda Pkwy.

GPS Coordinates: 39.7083° N, 104.8233° W

Nearest Town: Aurora

Interesting Facts: The museum hosts diverse programming like tours, lectures, and hands-on school programs, making history fun for all ages.

BOULDER

Pearl Street Mall

Why You Should Visit: As Boulder's vibrant pedestrian hub, Pearl Street Mall bursts with the city's spirited culture. Historic buildings now house unique boutiques and eateries with alfresco dining. Street performers entertain passersby, while events and festivals enliven the bricks year-round. On Pearl Street, you can shop for local artisan wares, sample the food scene, browse galleries, or simply soak up the lively ambience of downtown Boulder.

Best Time to Visit: Spring through fall, when weather is ideal for strolling and outdoor dining, and street performers are in full swing.

Location: Pearl St, Boulder, CO

Directions: From Denver, take US-36 W to Boulder, exit towards Downtown Boulder, follow Canyon Blvd to Pearl St.

GPS Coordinates: 40.0181° N, 105.2795° W

Nearest Town: Boulder

Interesting Facts: Pearl Street hosts a variety of happenings annually, like Bands on the Bricks concerts and the popular Boulder County Farmers Market.

Boulder Flatirons

Why You Should Visit: Boulder's signature landmark, the Flatirons rock formations, beckon outdoor enthusiasts with a spectacular natural playground of hiking amidst breathtaking scenery. Trails range from gentle rambles to challenging vertical ascents, letting you immerse in nature while testing your limits. Their heights offer stunning Boulder panoramas.

Best Time to Visit: Late spring through early fall when snow clears and mild weather prevails.

Location: Boulder Mountain Park, Boulder, CO

Directions: From downtown Boulder, head south on Broadway to Bluebell Road, following signs to Chautauqua Park, the gateway to the Flatirons.

GPS Coordinates: 39.9857° N, 105.2932° W

Nearest Town: Boulder

Interesting Facts: Pioneer women likened the angled rock formations to 19th-century irons, inspiring the name "Flatirons."

Chautauqua Park

Why You Should Visit: Chautauqua Park is the gateway to experiencing Boulder's natural majesty, from Flatirons panoramas to sprawling green spaces. Lush meadows set the scene for picnicking and soaking up vistas of the iconic rock formations, while dense trail networks let you hike directly into the mountains. Historical buildings dot the idyllic park, where you can appreciate both cultural and natural treasures.

Best Time to Visit: Accessible year-round, but ideal for hiking and picnicking from spring through fall.

Location: 900 Baseline Road, Boulder, CO

Directions: From Boulder, travel west on Baseline Road, following signs to Chautauqua Park.

GPS Coordinates: 39.9984° N, 105.2819° W

Nearest Town: Boulder

Interesting Facts: Home to the Colorado Chautauqua Association established in 1898, part of the nationwide Chautauqua Movement promoting education and community.

Boulder Creek Path

Why You Should Visit: The Boulder Creek Path is a beloved trail following the tranquil Boulder Creek through the heart of town. Its miles of paved path are perfect for cycling, jogging, or leisurely strolling past creekside parks, recreational spots, and natural beauty. Escape into serenity and scenery on this refreshing trail getaway right in Boulder.

Best Time to Visit: Spring through fall, when weather is ideal and foliage flourishing.

Location: The path runs through central Boulder alongside Boulder Creek.

Directions: Accessible from numerous points in Boulder; a popular starting point is Eben G. Fine Park.

GPS Coordinates: 40.0131° N, 105.2902° W (Eben G. Fine Park)

Nearest Town: Boulder

Interesting Facts: The path is part of the longer Boulder Creek Regional Trail, extending beyond town through countryside for more adventurous journeys.

Eldorado Canyon State Park

(8)

Why You Should Visit: Eldorado Canyon State Park is an outdoor adventurer's wonderland. Towering sandstone cliffs draw droves of rock climbers, while the park's many trails allow you to hike and bike through quintessential Colorado wilderness. South Boulder Creek's rushing waters provide a peaceful backdrop to active pursuits.

Best Time to Visit: Summer and fall for ideal climbing and hiking weather. In winter, snow-dusted cliffs and frozen waterfalls create a photogenic but chilly scene.

Location: 9 Kneale Rd, Eldorado Springs, CO 80025

Directions: From Boulder, take CO-93 S, turn right on CO-170 W/El Dorado Springs Dr and follow to the park.

GPS Coordinates: 39.9311° N, 105.2880° W

Nearest Town: Eldorado Springs

Interesting Facts: The park's cliffs boast over 500 technical climbing routes, making it a premier rock climbing destination.

BRECKENRIDGE

Breckenridge Ski Resort

Why You Should Visit: Breckenridge Ski Resort is a winter wonderland spanning five peaks and offering 187 trails for all skill levels. Skiers and snowboarders flock to its renowned slopes, from gentle runs for novices to challenging drops for experts. Soak up stunning alpine vistas as you carve through powder or relax at the base area. With extensive terrain, it's a haven for winter sports enthusiasts.

Best Time to Visit: Winter (November-April) for snow sports. Summer offers hiking and mountain biking.

Location: 1599 Ski Hill Rd, Breckenridge, CO

Directions: From Denver, take I-70 W to CO-9 S in Frisco, follow CO-9 S into Breckenridge.

GPS Coordinates: 39.4806° N, 106.0669° W

Nearest Town: Breckenridge

Interesting Facts: One of the Western Hemisphere's most-visited ski resorts, with a rich mining history dating to the 1800s.

Boreas Pass

Why You Should Visit: At 11,482 feet, Boreas Pass offers unmatched panoramas of the Rocky Mountains. The scenic route follows a historic railroad bed, whisking you through aspens and wildflower meadows. It's a high-elevation window into Colorado's wilderness.

Best Time to Visit: From June to September when snow has melted and the pass is accessible.

Location: Boreas Pass Road, Breckenridge, CO

Directions: From Breckenridge, head east on Wellington Road, turn left on French Street, right on Boreas Pass Road.

GPS Coordinates: 39.4104° N, 106.0193° W

Nearest Town: Breckenridge

Interesting Facts: The pass served miners and settlers in the 1800s before becoming a railroad route. It's now a beautiful drive and cycling path.

Edwin Carter Discovery Center

Why You Should Visit: As a treasure trove for history buffs, the Edwin Carter Discovery Center's 1875 museum home transports you back in time to explore the intriguing life and work of Edwin Carter, a miner turned passionate taxidermist and naturalist who dedicated himself to the wildlife of Colorado.

Best Time to Visit: From June to October when Breckenridge's weather is at its peak for exploring.

Location: 111 N Ridge St, Breckenridge, CO

Directions: From Main Street in Breckenridge, turn onto Ridge Street. The Discovery Center is a short walk on the right.

GPS Coordinates: 39.4814° N, 106.0450° W

Nearest Town: Breckenridge

Interesting Facts: Edwin Carter's extensive collection was the genesis of the Denver Museum of Nature and Science, showcasing his enduring legacy in Colorado's natural history.

Breckenridge Isak Heartstone Troll

Why You Should Visit: Located just outside Breckenridge, the mammoth wood troll sculpture known as Isak Heartstone is a whimsical and larger-than-life photo opportunity not to be missed. Admire the intricate hand-carved detailing and massive 15-foot height of this mythical forest creature, spread joy by sitting on his gigantic fingers, and take silly selfies capturing Isak's sheer enormity.

Best Time to Visit: Year-round.

Location: Breckenridge, CO

Directions: From downtown Breckenridge, take Boreas Pass Rd and follow signs to the trailhead parking area. The short hike leads right to Isak.

GPS Coordinates: 39.4024° N, 106.1550° W

Nearest Town: Breckenridge, CO

Interesting Facts: Sculptor Thomas Dambo constructed Isak entirely from reclaimed wood to highlight sustainability and human connections.

McCullough Gulch Trail

Why You Should Visit: Feast your eyes on nature's beauty along the alpine jewel known as McCullough Gulch Trail, which leads avid hikers past rainbows of vibrant wildflowers and cascading waterfalls to finally arrive at a serenely picturesque lake surrounded by towering peaks - an ideal moderately challenging trail perfect for photographers and nature lovers seeking jaw-dropping vistas and peaceful mountain wilderness.

Best Time to Visit: From June to September when the trail is snow-free and wildflowers are blooming.

Location: McCullough Gulch Rd, Breckenridge, CO

Directions: From Breckenridge, take CO-9 S. Turn right on Blue Lakes Dr, then right on McCullough Gulch Rd to the trailhead.

GPS Coordinates: 39.4050° N, 106.0619° W

Nearest Town: Breckenridge

Interesting Facts: Part of the White River National Forest, one of America's most visited forests spanning 2.3 million rugged alpine acres.

CAÑON CITY

Royal Gorge Bridge and Park

Why You Should Visit: The Royal Gorge Bridge and Park is an engineering marvel surrounded by natural splendor. The bridge suspends awe-inspiringly high above the Arkansas River as the highest in the US. Adrenaline activities like a bridge-spanning zipline and canyon-swinging skycoaster thrill adventure seekers.

Best Time to Visit: From May through September when weather's ideal and all attractions are open.

Location: 4218 Co Rd 3A, Cañon City, CO

Directions: From Cañon City, head west on US-50 W, turn right on Co Rd 3A, follow signs.

GPS Coordinates: 38.4610° N, 105.3249° W

Nearest Town: Cañon City

Interesting Facts: The Royal Gorge Bridge held the world's highest suspension bridge title from 1929 to 2001.

Skyline Drive

Why You Should Visit: Skyline Drive offers an exhilarating driving experience along a narrow, winding ridge-top road with panoramic views of Cañon City and the surrounding scenery. This historic route built by 20th century prison inmates provides a thrilling, daring drive with scenic pull-offs.

Best Time to Visit: Spring or fall when weather is clear and the views are spectacular.

Location: Skyline Dr, Cañon City, CO

Directions: From Cañon City, head west on US-50 W, turn left on CR-3, then sharp right onto Skyline Drive.

GPS Coordinates: 38.4495° N, 105.2352° W

Nearest Town: Cañon City

Interesting Facts: Though only 3 miles long, the heart-pumping one-way drive features sheer drops on each side.

Temple Canyon Park

Why You Should Visit: Nestled within a rugged canyon, Temple Canyon Park is a hidden gem offering tranquility and natural beauty. Legend has it the unique Temple Canyon served as a shelter for Ute Indians. Hiking trails to the natural amphitheater provide splendid views, making this a great spot to explore the outdoors.

Best Time to Visit: From late spring through early fall when the weather is warm and trails are easily accessible.

Location: Temple Canyon Rd, Cañon City, CO

Directions: From Cañon City, head south on S 9th St, continue onto Temple Canyon Rd to the entrance.

GPS Coordinates: 38.3644° N, 105.2282° W

Nearest Town: Cañon City

Interesting Facts: The canyon's natural amphitheater creates an echo, evoking a temple-like aura that named the park.

COLORADO SPRINGS

Garden of the Gods

(9)

Why You Should Visit: Recognized for its towering sandstone formations against snow-capped Pikes Peak, Garden of the Gods is nature's artistry on grand display. Hike among the surreal rock sculptures, climb the dizzying sandstone cliffs, or simply soak in the majestic vistas. However you choose to experience it, this park promises a rejuvenating and thrilling escape.

Best Time to Visit: Spring or fall, when mild weather prevails and crowds are smaller.

Location: 1805 N 30th St, Colorado Springs, CO

Directions: In Colorado Springs, head west on W Colorado Ave toward N Cascade Ave, turn right on N 30th St. The entrance is on the right.

GPS Coordinates: 38.8814° N, 104.8854° W

Nearest Town: Colorado Springs

Interesting Facts: In 1859, surveyors thought it would be a great spot for a beer garden, but deemed it a place fit for the gods to gather.

Pikes Peak

Why You Should Visit: Nicknamed "America's Mountain," Pikes Peak offers stunning 360° views that inspired the anthem "America the Beautiful." Towering over 14,000 feet, it lures hikers, drivers, and train riders to experience its majestic summit. Reach the top by scenic highway, on foot, or via the cog railway for an unforgettable alpine panorama.

Best Time to Visit: Late spring to early summer offers warmer weather and minimal chance of snow.

Location: Pikes Peak, Colorado 80809

Directions: From Colorado Springs, take US-24 W, follow signs to access Pikes Peak Highway, hiking trails, or the cog railway.

GPS Coordinates: 38.8409° N, 105.0442° W

Nearest Town: Colorado Springs

Interesting Facts: One of Colorado's 53 fourteeners, Pikes Peak is the world's 2nd most visited mountain after Japan's Mount Fuji.

Cheyenne Mountain Zoo

Why You Should Visit: Perched at an elevation, Cheyenne Mountain Zoo blends wildlife encounters with stunning city views. It boasts the largest herd of giraffes in the U.S., interactive exhibits, and conservation efforts.

Blending fun, learning, and awe, a day here is a uniquely Colorado zoo experience.

Best Time to Visit: Spring and early summer when the weather's pleasant and animals are active.

Location: 4250 Cheyenne Mountain Zoo Rd, Colorado Springs, CO

Directions: From downtown Colorado Springs, head southwest on W Colorado Ave, follow signs to the zoo 6 miles away.

GPS Coordinates: 38.7711° N, 104.8534° W

Nearest Town: Colorado Springs

Interesting Facts: As the nation's only mountainside zoo, it offers a one-of-a-kind wildlife experience with scenic views.

The Broadmoor Seven Falls

Why You Should Visit: The Broadmoor Seven Falls is a breathtaking series of cascading waterfalls within a narrow canyon where the grandeur of water meets rock. This natural spectacle offers a tranquil yet awe-inspiring setting. Surrounding trails and zip lines provide adventurous ways to experience the majestic falls up close.

Best Time to Visit: Late spring to early summer, when water flow peaks and foliage flourishes.

Location: 1045 Lower Gold Camp Rd, Colorado Springs, CO

Directions: From Colorado Springs, take W Cimarron St and S 21st St to Lower Gold Camp Rd, follow to Seven Falls.

GPS Coordinates: 38.7897° N, 104.8706° W

Nearest Town: Colorado Springs

Interesting Facts: Dubbed "The Grandest Mile of Scenery in Colorado", Seven Falls packs stunning natural beauty into an accessible space.

Cave of the Winds Mountain Park

Why You Should Visit: Cave of the Winds is a hidden subterranean treasure, offering a glimpse into ancient geological formations. From illuminating cave tours to thrill rides like the Terror-Dactyl canyon plunge, it blends education with excitement. Guided tours reveal stunning stalactites, stalagmites, and more.

Best Time to Visit: Spring through fall for mild weather, although it's open year-round.

Location: 100 Cave of the Winds Rd, Manitou Springs, CO

Directions: From Colorado Springs, follow W Colorado Ave and Manitou Ave to Cave of the Winds Rd in Manitou Springs, continue to destination.

GPS Coordinates: 38.8721° N, 104.9142° W

Nearest Town: Manitou Springs

Interesting Facts: Discovered in 1881, it's been a must-see attraction for geology and adventure fans since.

COMANCHE NATIONAL GRASSLAND

Comanche National Grassland

Why You Should Visit: The expansive Comanche National Grassland transports you to a simpler time. Its vast plains and rich archaeological sites provide a window into ancient history. Explore dinosaur tracks, hike pristine prairies, and revel in the tranquility of untouched natural beauty.

Best Time to Visit: Spring (April-June) or fall (September-October) offer mild weather with fewer crowds.

Location: Comanche National Grassland, Colorado

Directions: Accessible from various entry points, but commonly via US-160 E from Trinidad, CO.

GPS Coordinates: 37.4250° N, 103.3342° W

Nearest Towns: Trinidad or La Junta, CO

Interesting Facts: Home to the longest dinosaur trackway in North America, connecting visitors to prehistoric times.

DENVER

Red Rocks Amphitheatre

(10)

Why You Should Visit: More than just a venue, the iconic Red Rocks Amphitheatre is an awe-inspiring natural phenomenon. Dramatic 70-million-year-old red rock formations set the scene for an unparalleled concert-going experience. This acoustic marvel has hosted famous acts through the decades, serenaded by stars and geology.

Best Time to Visit: Summer season from May to September when most events are held.

Location: 18300 W Alameda Pkwy, Morrison, CO

Directions: From Denver, take I-70 W to exit 259 for Morrison, follow signs.

GPS Coordinates: 39.6656° N, 105.2056° W

Nearest Town: Morrison, CO

Interesting Facts: It's the only naturally occurring, acoustically perfect amphitheater in the world.

Denver Art Museum

Why You Should Visit: The Denver Art Museum (DAM) is a haven for art lovers, housing over 70,000 works spanning centuries and continents. It boasts renowned collections of Native American, Western American, and European/Asian art. The bold architectural designs are artworks in themselves, blending urban life with Colorado's natural splendor.

Best Time to Visit: Year-round, though weekdays are less crowded.

Location: 100 W 14th Ave Pkwy, Denver, CO

Directions: Located downtown and easily accessible via Speer Blvd or Broadway St, with ample nearby parking.

GPS Coordinates: 39.7361° N, 104.9897° W

Nearest Town: Denver, CO

Interesting Facts: The Hamilton Building's peaks mimic Colorado's mountains and rock crystals, seamlessly integrating art and nature.

Denver Botanic Gardens

Why You Should Visit: A peaceful oasis in the city's heart, Denver Botanic Gardens offers a diverse botanical collection across thoughtfully designed gardens and tranquil ponds. Experience beauty, education, and conservation in this urban sanctuary for nature lovers. Special events and programs promote botany year-round.

Best Time to Visit: Spring to early summer when flowers burst into bloom, though seasonal displays enchant year-round.

Location: 1007 York St, Denver, CO

Directions: Accessible via E 9th Ave and York St, with onsite parking.

GPS Coordinates: 39.7323° N, 104.9603° W

Nearest Town: Denver, CO

Interesting Facts: The iconic 1960s Boettcher Memorial Tropical Conservatory evokes a rainforest environment to house exotic plants.

Denver Zoo

Why You Should Visit: Home to over 4,000 animals across 600 species, Denver Zoo offers an immersive window into the wonders of wildlife. Get up close with creatures from around the globe in naturalistic habitats aimed at education and conservation. Special events and animal babies debut in spring, but the zoo enthralls year-round.

Best Time to Visit: Spring and fall for pleasant weather, while spring welcomes newborn animals.

Location: 2300 Steele St, Denver, CO

Directions: Located in City Park, accessible via Colorado Blvd to 23rd Ave, following signs. Parking onsite.

GPS Coordinates: 39.7504° N, 104.9485° W

Nearest Town: Denver, CO

Interesting Facts: The zoo's expansive Toyota Elephant Passage habitat highlights its commitment to conservation and sustainability.

Larimer Square

Why You Should Visit: As Denver's most historic block, Larimer Square recounts the city's past while embracing the present. Charming historic buildings now house chic boutiques, clubs, and restaurants. With twinkling lights and nostalgic ambiance, it blends old and new for delightful strolls day or night.

Best Time to Visit: Lovely year-round, but especially lively in spring/summer with plentiful outdoor dining and energy.

Location: Larimer St, between 14th and 15th streets, Denver, CO

Directions: Located downtown and accessible by car or transit, with nearby parking options.

GPS Coordinates: 39.7472° N, 104.9995° W

Nearest Town: Denver, CO

Interesting Facts: Founded by Denver's founder William Larimer, its preservation pioneered urban revitalization in the US.

Union Station

Why You Should Visit: More than a transit hub, Denver's Union Station is a vibrant locale filled with boutiques, eateries, and a hotel. Its blend of historic charm and modern amenities makes it ideal for dining, shopping, or simply soaking in the lively ambience. It seamlessly fuses the city's heritage with its cosmopolitan spirit.

Best Time to Visit: A year-round destination, but the holiday season brings special charm with festive decor and events.

Location: 1701 Wynkoop St, Denver, CO

Directions: At Wynkoop and 17th streets downtown, accessible via buses, light rail, and other transit.

GPS Coordinates: 39.7531° N, 104.9997° W

Nearest Town: Denver, CO

Interesting Facts: Originally opened in 1881, it has long served as a key transportation hub in the western US.

DINOSAUR

Dinosaur National Monument

Why You Should Visit: Step into prehistory at Dinosaur National Monument, a trove of ancient fossils including well-preserved dino bones. Beyond the primeval relics, the rugged landscape harbors petroglyphs and scenic river canyons for a blend of natural and ancient wonders.

Best Time to Visit: Late spring through early fall offers pleasant temperatures and snow-free trails.

Location: Dinosaur, CO

Directions: Accessible from Colorado and Utah. Follow signs to visitor centers from Dinosaur, CO or Jensen, UT.

GPS Coordinates: 40.4924° N, 108.9416° W

Nearest Town: Dinosaur, CO

Interesting Facts: The Quarry Exhibit Hall allows you to view roughly 1,500 dinosaur bones in an enclosed area!

DURANGO

Durango & Silverton Narrow Gauge Railroad

Why You Should Visit: This vintage steam train transports you back in time, replicating old west travel through the picturesque San Juan Mountains. More than just a ride, it's a scenic marvel and living history lesson in one unforgettable journey.

Best Time to Visit: Summer's warm, sunny weather optimizes enjoying the breathtaking scenery.

Location: 479 Main Avenue, Durango, CO

Directions: The depot is centrally located in downtown Durango. From the north, take US-550 S to Main Ave. From the south, take US-160 W and US-550 N to Main Ave.

GPS Coordinates: 37.2753° N, 107.8800667° W

Nearest Town: Durango, CO

Interesting Facts: In continuous operation since 1882, it shuttled people and goods between Durango and Silverton despite the San Juans' harsh conditions.

Animas River Trail

Why You Should Visit: Traversing alongside the pristine Animas River, this trail offers serene yet invigorating walks, runs, and bike rides flanked by beautiful water views and natural scenery. Accessing parks and open spaces, it's a cherished outdoor gem in Durango.

Best Time to Visit: Spring through fall brings mild weather and the trail's peak natural splendor.

Location: Durango, CO

Directions: Accessible from various Durango points, like the 9th Street Bridge.

GPS Coordinates: 37.2737° N, 107.8816° W

Nearest Town: Durango, CO

Interesting Facts: The 7-mile paved pathway connects to trails including the 500+ mile Colorado Trail from Denver to Durango.

San Juan National Forest

Why You Should Visit: The sprawling San Juan National Forest is a natural wonderland near Durango. With sweeping wild landscapes, soaring peaks, serene lakes, and endless hiking trails, it's a paradise for outdoor enthusiasts. Immerse yourself in untouched beauty while hiking, camping, fishing, or simply reveling in the wilderness.

Best Time to Visit: Summer and fall offer pleasant weather and fall foliage, though it entices year-round.

Location: 15 Burnett Ct, Durango, CO

Directions: From Durango, head north on Main Ave, continuing on US-550 N. Follow signs.

GPS Coordinates: 37.4250° N, 107.8300° W

Nearest Town: Durango, CO

Interesting Facts: Encompassing over 1.8 million acres, it's a vast playground for nature and adventure lovers.

ESTES PARK

Rocky Mountain National Park

(11)

Why You Should Visit: Nestled near Estes Park, Rocky Mountain National Park is a crown jewel of Colorado's natural majesty. Over 265,000 acres of pristine wilderness, towering peaks, diverse wildlife, and 300+ miles of trails create a haven for nature and adventure lovers. Its stunning vistas, observed along scenic drives or while hiking, stay with you long after departing.

Best Time to Visit: Summer and early fall offer pleasant weather and clear trails, ideal for exploration.

Location: Estes Park, CO

Directions: From Estes Park, follow US-36 W to the park entrance.

GPS Coordinates: 40.3428° N, 105.6836° W

Nearest Town: Estes Park, CO

Interesting Facts: Home to Trail Ridge Road, the highest continuous paved road in the US, boasting breathtaking mountain views.

Estes Park Aerial Tramway

Why You Should Visit: The Estes Park Aerial Tramway offers a unique way to admire the area's beauty, whisking you up Prospect Mountain for panoramic views of Rocky Mountain National Park and the charming town below. This engineering marvel blends scenic splendor with an unforgettable ride.

Best Time to Visit: Summer, late May through early September when the tramway operates, allowing you to escape the heat while enjoying sunny days.

Location: 420 E Riverside Dr, Estes Park, CO

Directions: From downtown, head southeast on Big Thompson Ave, turn right on E Riverside Dr. It's on the right.

GPS Coordinates: 40.3701° N, 105.5083° W

Nearest Town: Estes Park, CO

Interesting Facts: Designed and built by renowned aerial tramway engineer Robert Heron.

The Stanley Hotel

Why You Should Visit: More than lodging, The Stanley Hotel is a journey into history and the paranormal. This icon inspired Stephen King's "The Shining" and offers stunning mountain vistas. With historical architecture, beautiful surroundings, and rumored ghostly residents, it's an adventure unto itself.

Best Time to Visit: Fall showcases autumn colors, but spring and summer boast lush landscapes. Ghost tours and events year-round.

Location: 333 E Wonderview Ave, Estes Park, CO

Directions: From downtown Estes Park, head northeast on Big Thompson Ave, turn left on Marys Lake Rd, right on Wonderview Ave.

GPS Coordinates: 40.3772° N, 105.5192° W

Nearest Town: Estes Park, CO

Interesting Facts: Renowned for haunting charm, it's a must for paranormal intrigue. The ghost tours are famous!

Trail Ridge Road

Why You Should Visit: Trail Ridge Road is a journey through the clouds, as the highest continuous paved road in the US. It rewards with breathtaking Rocky Mountain vistas, overlooks, and pull-offs for awe-inspiring photos. This engineering marvel is the gateway to experiencing Rocky Mountain National Park's majesty.

Best Time to Visit: Late May through mid-October when the road is typically clear of snow.

Location: Rocky Mountain National Park, CO

Directions: From Estes Park, enter the park via Beaver Meadows Entrance and follow signs for Trail Ridge Road/US-34 W.

GPS Coordinates: 40.3554° N, 105.6975° W

Nearest Town: Estes Park, CO

Interesting Facts: At 12,183 feet, its highest point offers an almost celestial view of the Rockies and valleys below.

FORT COLLINS

Horsetooth Reservoir

Why You Should Visit: Horsetooth Reservoir is a haven for outdoor enthusiasts with its clear waters encircled by rolling hills. A prime spot for boating, fishing, swimming and hiking, its picturesque setting sweetens the natural retreat from city life.

Best Time to Visit: Summer months from June through August for water activities. Spring and fall offer beauty with fewer crowds.

Location: West of Fort Collins, CO

Directions: From Fort Collins, take Harmony Road west to County Road 38 E. Follow signs to the reservoir.

GPS Coordinates: 40.5569° N, 105.1817° W

Nearest Town: Fort Collins, CO

Interesting Facts: Named after the tooth-shaped Horsetooth Mountain, part of local folklore.

Fort Collins Museum of Discovery

Why You Should Visit: The Fort Collins Museum of Discovery blends history, science, and culture through interactive exhibits. Explore the region's heritage, natural wonders, and more through engaging displays. With something for all ages, it makes for a fun family outing.

Best Time to Visit: Year-round, though weekdays have fewer crowds.

Location: 408 Mason Court, Fort Collins, CO

Directions: From downtown Fort Collins, head north on College Ave, turn left on Cherry St, right on Mason Ct.

GPS Coordinates: 40.5936° N, 105.0807° W

Nearest Town: Fort Collins, CO

Interesting Facts: The Digital Dome Theater immerses you in mesmerizing films and visual adventures.

Cache La Poudre River

Why You Should Visit: Famed for pristine waters and abundant outdoor options, the Cache La Poudre River has something for every nature lover. Whitewater raft, fish, hike or simply relax along its serene natural surroundings.

Best Time to Visit: Late spring to early summer for rafting, fall for fishing.

Location: Flows through Roosevelt National Forest near Fort Collins, CO.

Directions: From Fort Collins, take US-287 N to Ted's Place, turn left on CO-14 W into the Poudre Canyon area.

GPS Coordinates: 40.6914° N, 105.6190° W

Nearest Town: Fort Collins, CO

Interesting Facts: "Cache la Poudre" means "hide the powder" in French, referring to trappers burying gunpowder in its banks during a snowstorm.

GLENWOOD SPRINGS

Glenwood Hot Springs Pool

Why You Should Visit: As one of the world's largest natural hot springs pools, Glenwood Hot Springs Pool is a haven of relaxation against beautiful mountain views. Soak away your cares year-round in the tranquil, heated waters.

Best Time to Visit: Appealing year-round, but especially charming to soak amid winter snowfall.

Location: 401 N River St, Glenwood Springs, CO

Directions: From I-70, take exit 116, head north following signs.

GPS Coordinates: 39.5509° N, 107.3243° W

Nearest Town: Glenwood Springs, CO

Interesting Facts: Ute Indians first enjoyed the healing waters, which have drawn visitors since 1888.

Hanging Lake

Why You Should Visit: A geological marvel and iconic Colorado hike, Hanging Lake enchants with its pristine waters encircled by lush foliage and cascading falls. For nature lovers, its ethereal setting promises an otherworldly experience.

Best Time to Visit: Late spring to early summer when the trail is snow-free and greenery flourishes.

Location: Glenwood Canyon, Glenwood Springs, CO

Directions: From Glenwood Springs, take I-70 E to Exit 125. Park at the rest area to begin your hike.

GPS Coordinates: 39.6014° N, 107.1916° W

Nearest Town: Glenwood Springs, CO

Interesting Facts: Swimming and touching the delicate waters are prohibited to preserve the lake's natural splendor.

Glenwood Caverns Adventure Park

Why You Should Visit: Blending thrill and natural beauty, Glenwood Caverns Adventure Park offers cave tours plus daring rides atop a mountain for a unique mix of wonder and excitement. Experience natural caves and heart-pounding fun under sunny skies.

Best Time to Visit: Summer and fall for ideal weather to enjoy the attractions.

Location: 51000 Two Rivers Plaza Road, Glenwood Springs, CO

Directions: From Glenwood Springs, head west on I-70, take exit 116, continue on N River Dr, turn on Devereux Rd, then Two Rivers Plaza Rd.

GPS Coordinates: 39.5515° N, 107.3254° W

Nearest Town: Glenwood Springs, CO

Interesting Facts: Home to America's only mountain-top theme park with thrilling rides and jaw-dropping Colorado views.

GOLDEN

Lookout Mountain

Why You Should Visit: Lookout Mountain blends history, natural beauty, and sweeping Golden views. Home to the Buffalo Bill Museum and Grave honoring the Wild West legend, it offers a mix of frontier heritage and panoramic vistas.

Best Time to Visit: Spring through fall for pleasant outdoor weather.

Location: 987 Lookout Mountain Road, Golden, CO

Directions: From downtown Golden, take the Lariat Loop Scenic & Historic Byway leading straight to Lookout Mountain.

GPS Coordinates: 39.7325° N, 105.2392° W

Nearest Town: Golden, CO

Interesting Facts: Buffalo Bill chose Lookout Mountain as his final resting place, now a popular gravesite.

Coors Brewery

Why You Should Visit: Iconic for beer aficionados, Golden's Coors Brewery is the world's largest single-site facility, offering insightful tours with complimentary tastings. Learn about Coors' rich brewing history and process before sampling beers for visitors 21+.

Best Time to Visit: Anytime, though spring through fall allows outdoor sipping.

Location: 13th & Ford Street, Golden, CO

Directions: From Denver, take I-70 W, exit 265 for CO-58 W to Golden/Central City, continue on CO-58 W, take Washington Ave to Ford St.

GPS Coordinates: 39.7532° N, 105.2231° W

Nearest Town: Golden, CO

Interesting Facts: Coors has been brewing in Golden for over 140 years, integral to Colorado's beer culture.

Golden Gate Canyon State Park

Why You Should Visit: A natural haven near Golden, Golden Gate Canyon State Park boasts over 12,000 acres of forests, rocky peaks, and aspen meadows perfect for hiking, wildlife viewing, picnicking, and horseback riding. Numerous scenic trails offer stunning vistas, including the Continental Divide stretching 100 miles.

Best Time to Visit: Spring through fall for ideal outdoor weather.

Location: 92 Crawford Gulch Rd, Golden, CO

Directions: From Golden, head north on Washington Ave, continue on CO-93 N, turn left on Golden Gate Canyon Rd, right on Crawford Gulch Rd.

GPS Coordinates: 39.8719° N, 105.4170° W

Nearest Town: Golden, CO

Interesting Facts: Unique rustic "yurt" lodging offers an overnight wilderness experience.

Buffalo Bill Museum and Grave

Why You Should Visit: Gain insight into William "Buffalo Bill" Cody at this museum and gravesite. Browse Cody memorabilia in the museum, then pay respects at his scenic mountainside resting place. Together, they illuminate the icon's frontier life.

Best Time to Visit: Spring through fall for pleasant weather while exploring.

Location: 987 1/2 Lookout Mountain Road, Golden, CO

Directions: From downtown Golden, take US-40 W, continue onto Lookout Mountain Road, follow signs.

GPS Coordinates: 39.7324° N, 105.2384° W

Nearest Town: Golden, CO

Interesting Facts: Buffalo Bill gained fame for his Wild West shows, which romanticized frontier living across the US and Europe.

GRAND JUNCTION

Colorado National Monument

(12)

Why You Should Visit: Boasting majestic canyons and soaring monoliths, Colorado National Monument stuns with surreal landscapes perfect for hiking, biking, and wildlife viewing. Lose yourself in the wonder of this natural masterpiece.

Best Time to Visit: Spring (April-May) and fall (September-October) offer mild weather with fewer crowds.

Location: 1750 Rim Rock Drive, Fruita, CO

Directions: From Grand Junction, head west on I-70W, exit 19 to Fruita, turn left on CO-340E, follow signs.

GPS Coordinates: 39.0575° N, 108.6939° W

Nearest Town: Fruita, CO

Interesting Facts: The 23-mile scenic Rim Rock Drive rewards with breathtaking canyon and valley views.

Museum of the West

Why You Should Visit: The Museum of the West offers an immersion into the rich, diverse history of Western Colorado, from ancient cultures to the Wild West era. A treasure trove of artifacts and exhibits transports you through time.

Best Time to Visit: A great indoor activity year-round, especially during colder months.

Location: 462 Ute Ave, Grand Junction, CO

Directions: From I-70, take exit 37 to Clifton, head west on I-70BL W, continue on US-6 W, turn right on N 5th St, left on Ute Ave.

GPS Coordinates: 39.0681° N, 108.5633° W

Nearest Town: Grand Junction, CO

Interesting Facts: Don't miss the panoramic valley views from the tower.

Downtown Grand Junction

Why You Should Visit: Downtown Grand Junction delights with charming boutiques, eateries, and art galleries amid tree-lined streets. Outdoor sculptures, a friendly ambiance, and lively events like markets and festivals make it a vibrant hub to explore.

Best Time to Visit: Spring through fall to enjoy pleasant weather, outdoor art, and street fairs.

Location: Main St, Grand Junction, CO

Directions: From I-70, take exit 37 to Clifton, continue on I-70BL W/US-6 W, turn right on N 1st St, left on Main St.

GPS Coordinates: 39.0675° N, 108.5700° W

Nearest Town: Grand Junction, CO

Interesting Facts: A cultural hotspot, downtown hosts farmers' markets, music festivals, and art strolls.

GREAT SAND DUNES NATIONAL PARK

Great Sand Dunes National Park

Why You Should Visit: North America's tallest dunes offer surreal landscapes for hiking, sledding, and photography. Their stunning juxtaposition against wetlands and alpine peaks is a sight to behold. Visit when Medano Creek flows for a unique beach-like experience.

Best Time to Visit: Late spring to early summer for optimal creek flow.

Location: 11999 State Highway 150, Mosca, CO

Directions: From Denver, take I-25 S, US-160 W, CO-150 N.

GPS Coordinates: 37.7916° N, 105.5943° W

Nearest Town: Alamosa, CO

Interesting Facts: Formed from Rio Grande sand deposits, the dunes accumulated over time as winds sweeping the valley lost power before the Sangre de Cristo Range.

GUNNISON

Black Canyon of the Gunnison National Park

Why You Should Visit: A testament to erosion's force, Black Canyon's sheer cliffs and narrow depths carved by the Gunnison River stun the eye. Take in dramatic vistas and dark canyon walls on drives, hikes, and climbs.

Best Time to Visit: Late spring through early fall offers pleasant weather and open roads/trails.

Location: 9800 Hwy 347, Gunnison, CO

Directions: From Gunnison, take US-50 W, then CO-347 north for 14 miles.

GPS Coordinates: 38.5754° N, -107.7416° W

Nearest Town: Gunnison, CO

Interesting Facts: Parts of the steep, narrow gorge get just 33 minutes of sunlight a day - hence the name Black Canyon.

LEADVILLE

Leadville Colorado & Southern Railroad

Why You Should Visit: More than transit, the Leadville Colorado & Southern Railroad transports you back in time on scenic Rocky Mountain rides. Soak in breathtaking views while learning Leadville's rich mining history for an engaging blend of nature, heritage, and adventure.

Best Time to Visit: Summer months, June through August, when daily operations allow scenic trips in ideal weather.

Location: 326 E 7th St, Leadville, CO

Directions: From downtown Leadville, head east on E 7th St. The station is a few blocks away.

GPS Coordinates: 39.2494° N, -106.2915° W

Nearest Town: Leadville, CO

Interesting Facts: Enjoy unique views of Colorado's highest peaks, Mount Elbert and Mount Massive. A photographer's dream!

National Mining Hall of Fame and Museum

Why You Should Visit: Immerse yourself in Colorado's rich mining heritage at this tribute to the industry's history and pioneers. Vast collections of artifacts, minerals, and engaging exhibits relay the significance of mining's past and its role in America's development.

Best Time to Visit: Open year-round, though summer/fall from June to October provides pleasant Leadville weather.

Location: 120 W 9th St, Leadville, CO

Directions: From downtown Leadville, drive or walk west to W 9th St.

GPS Coordinates: 39.2509° N, -106.2930° W

Nearest Town: Leadville, CO

Interesting Facts: Features a replica mining drift, offering an underground glimpse into historic mining life.

Turquoise Lake

Why You Should Visit: Turquoise Lake is a serene haven with crystalline waters and mountain vistas, perfect for camping, fishing, hiking, and appreciating Colorado's beauty. Its fittingly turquoise waters provide a peaceful setting for photography and boating.

Best Time to Visit: Summer months, June-August, offer warm weather and the open scenic drive.

Location: Leadville, CO

Directions: From Leadville, drive west on County Road 4, continue to County Road 9, follow signs.

GPS Coordinates: 39.2844° N, -106.4396° W

Nearest Town: Leadville, CO

Interesting Facts: The lake gets its name from the stunning turquoise hue its waters acquire under Colorado's sunny skies.

MANITOU SPRINGS

The Manitou Incline

Why You Should Visit: The Manitou Incline challenges fitness lovers, with its nearly 1-mile length gaining almost 2,000 feet in elevation. This steep former railway-turned-hiking trail provides a heart-pumping workout rewarded by awe-inspiring summit views.

Best Time to Visit: Spring through fall for pleasant weather, aiming for early/late in the day during summer.

Location: Manitou Springs, CO

Directions: From Colorado Springs, take US-24 W to Manitou Ave. Head to Ruxton Ave, follow signs.

GPS Coordinates: 38.8561° N, -104.9314° W

Nearest Town: Manitou Springs, CO

Interesting Facts: With punishing sections over 60% grade, the incline is an extreme test of endurance.

Manitou Cliff Dwellings

Why You Should Visit: Step back 800 years at these carefully preserved Anasazi cliff dwellings, offering a rare window into Native American life. Relocated from McElmo Canyon, these archaeological marvels let you explore the structures and learn about Anasazi culture through immersive history.

Best Time to Visit: Open year-round; spring and fall have pleasant weather.

Location: 10 Cliff Dwellings Rd, Manitou Springs, CO

Directions: From US-24 W, turn right on Cliff Dwellings Road, follow signs.

GPS Coordinates: 38.8675° N, -104.9172° W

Nearest Town: Manitou Springs, CO

Interesting Facts: The neighboring museum houses Anasazi artifacts, and the gift shop offers Native American arts and crafts.

Penny Arcade

Why You Should Visit: Manitou Springs' Penny Arcade offers a nostalgic trip playing vintage and modern arcade games. As the name suggests, many still cost only a penny! Relive childhood memories or make new ones with family and friends at this historic, budget-friendly arcade.

Best Time to Visit: Open year-round indoors, but avoid crowds on weekends/holidays.

Location: 900 Manitou Ave, Manitou Springs, CO

Directions: From US-24 W, take Manitou Ave exit, head east. It's on the right.

GPS Coordinates: 38.8575° N, -104.9177° W

Nearest Town: Manitou Springs, CO

Interesting Facts: This antique arcade is one of the country's oldest, with games dating back to the early 1900s.

MESA VERDE

Mesa Verde National Park

Why You Should Visit: A mesmerizing window into the past, Mesa Verde unveils some of America's best-preserved Ancestral Puebloan sites. With over 5,000 archaeological sites including 600 cliff dwellings, it's like stepping back in time. Must-see dwellings include Cliff Palace, Balcony House, and Long House for a glimpse of ancient life.

Best Time to Visit: Spring (April-May) and fall (September-October) offer pleasant weather with fewer crowds.

Location: Mesa Verde, CO

Directions: From U.S. Highway 160, turn onto CO-10 (Mesa Top Ruins Road) and follow signs.

GPS Coordinates: 37.2309° N, 108.4618° W

Nearest Town: Cortez, CO

Interesting Facts: A UNESCO World Heritage Site recognized for its superbly preserved ancient Native American dwellings.

MOUNT EVANS

Mount Evans Scenic Byway

Why You Should Visit: As America's highest paved road, Mount Evans Scenic Byway ascends to 14,130 feet with stunning Rocky Mountain views. Experience high-altitude splendor with alpine lakes, diverse wildlife, and heavenly vistas surrounding you as you drive.

Best Time to Visit: The byway is typically open Memorial Day weekend through Labor Day, but check road status before visiting.

Location: Mount Evans, CO

Directions: From Denver, take I-70 W to Exit 240 in Idaho Springs, follow CO-103 S/Chicago Creek Rd and CO-5 E to Mount Evans Rd.

GPS Coordinates: 39.5883° N, 105.6438° W

Nearest Town: Idaho Springs, CO

Interesting Facts: You can summit Mount Evans by hiking; despite the challenge, the 360° views are spectacular.

PAGOSA SPRINGS

Pagosa Hot Springs

Why You Should Visit: The soothing, mineral-rich waters of Pagosa Hot Springs offer relaxation and rejuvenation. Nestled along the San Juan River, these natural springs provide a serene soak amid Colorado's picturesque landscape. The contrast of warm waters and crisp air makes fall and winter visits especially magical.

Best Time to Visit: Enjoyable year-round, with fall/winter contrast particularly special.

Location: Pagosa Springs, CO

Directions: In downtown Pagosa Springs, easily accessible from US-160.

GPS Coordinates: 37.2694° N, 107.0098° W

Nearest Town: Pagosa Springs, CO

Interesting Facts: "Pagosa" means "boiling waters" in Native American languages, emphasizing the springs' therapeutic nature.

San Juan River Walk

Why You Should Visit: The tranquil San Juan River Walk invites leisurely strolls, jogs, or bike rides alongside the peaceful San Juan River. With benches, picnic spots, and plenty of places to admire the serene views, it's a soothing natural retreat.

Best Time to Visit: Spring and summer offer lush greenery, while fall brings spectacular autumn colors.

Location: Pagosa Springs, CO

Directions: Access from various Pagosa Springs points like Town Park on Hermosa Street.

GPS Coordinates: 37.2684° N, 107.0092° W

Nearest Town: Pagosa Springs, CO

Interesting Facts: The San Juan River, one of Colorado's longest, originates in the San Juan Mountains.

PALISADE

Chimney Rock National Monument

Why You Should Visit: A natural and historical marvel in the San Juan National Forest, Chimney Rock unveils ancient Puebloan ruins and insights into ancestral Pueblo culture. The iconic Chimney and Companion Rock formations are also stunning, especially under the full moon during special programs.

Best Time to Visit: May through September for pleasant weather and full moon viewings.

Location: Pagosa Springs, CO

Directions: From Pagosa Springs, take US-160 W, turn north on CO-151. Follow for about 20 miles.

GPS Coordinates: 37.1911° N, 107.2952° W

Nearest Town: Pagosa Springs, CO

Interesting Facts: During equinoxes, the moonrise aligns perfectly between the awe-inspiring rocks.

Colorado River State Park

Why You Should Visit: Colorado River State Park near Palisade offers picturesque scenery and bountiful outdoor activities. Fish, boat, picnic, or simply relax by the serene Colorado River for a peaceful escape in nature.

Best Time to Visit: Spring through fall has ideal weather and full amenities.

Location: Palisade, CO

Directions: From I-70, take exit 42 to Palisade. Merge onto 37 3/10 Rd, turn left on US-6 W. The entrance is on the right.

GPS Coordinates: 39.0917° N, 108.4618° W

Nearest Town: Palisade, CO

Interesting Facts: Palisade is renowned for its orchards and vineyards, making it a major Colorado fruit-growing region.

Palisade Rim Trail

Why You Should Visit: The Palisade Rim Trail is a hidden gem for hikers and bikers, with moderate to challenging terrain and breathtaking valley views. Its two loops reveal vistas of vineyards, the Colorado River, and the Grand Valley, offering a thrilling way to explore Colorado's diverse landscapes.

Best Time to Visit: Late spring through early fall has mild weather and clear, dry trails.

Location: Palisade, CO

Directions: From Palisade, head west on 3rd St, turn right on Elberta Ave, continue onto G 7/10 Rd, right on N River Rd. Follow signs to the trailhead.

GPS Coordinates: 39.1064° N, 108.3501° W

Nearest Town: Palisade, CO

Interesting Facts: The trail features ancient petroglyphs and rock art, linking to the region's Native American heritage.

Palisade Wine Country

Why You Should Visit: Dubbed Colorado's "Wine Capital," Palisade boasts award-winning wineries and a vibrant wine culture. Its unique terroir produces remarkable wines. Tasting vintages amid the scenic vineyards with majestic mountain backdrops is an experience wine lovers will treasure.

Best Time to Visit: Late summer through early fall to catch grape harvests and festivals celebrating local winemaking.

Location: 777 Grande River Drive, Palisade, CO

Directions: Wineries are scattered around Palisade, a short drive from Grand Junction. Follow the Fruit and Wine Byway.

GPS Coordinates: 39.1116° N, 108.3526° W

Nearest Town: Palisade, CO

Interesting Facts: Along with its famous wines, Palisade is renowned for its juicy, sweet peaches.

PUEBLO

Lake Pueblo State Park

Why You Should Visit: Lake Pueblo State Park is a water lover's paradise, with over 4,600 acres for boating, fishing, and water sports. Hiking and biking trails wind through the photogenic red rock formations and green shrubs of the surrounding land.

Best Time to Visit: Late spring through early fall offers warm weather perfect for water activities.

Location: 640 Pueblo Reservoir Road, Pueblo, CO

Directions: From downtown Pueblo, head west on US-50 W. Follow signs to the park, turning right on Pueblo Blvd, left on Thatcher Ave.

GPS Coordinates: 38.2550° N, 104.7286° W

Nearest Town: Pueblo, CO

Interesting Facts: Known as a prime "fishing hot spot" for diverse species like bass, catfish, and walleye.

Pueblo Zoo

Why You Should Visit: Nestled in Pueblo's historic City Park, the Pueblo Zoo is home to over 420 animals across 140+ species. Its intimate size, engaging exhibits like the Serengeti Safari, and Ecocenter provide educational, up-close animal encounters.

Best Time to Visit: Spring and fall for pleasant outdoor exploring. Summer sees animals most active.

Location: 3455 Nuckolls Ave, Pueblo, CO

Directions: From I-25 take exit 98B for City Center Dr, head to N Pueblo Blvd via Santa Fe Ave and W 8th St. Turn right on Goodnight Ave, left on Park Pl Ave.

GPS Coordinates: 38.254444° N, 104.621389° W

Nearest Town: Pueblo, CO

Interesting Facts: Founded in the 1920s, this century-old zoo lets visitors get remarkably close to learn about animals.

El Pueblo History Museum

Why You Should Visit: El Pueblo History Museum is a gateway into Colorado's rich cultural past, showcasing the convergence of Native American, Mexican, frontier, and early state influences. With unique exhibits and a replicated 1840s trading post, it brings regional history to life.

Best Time to Visit: Fall and spring allow comfortable outdoor exploration of the historic area.

Location: 301 N Union Ave, Pueblo, CO

Directions: From I-25 S take exit 98B for City Center Dr, head to N Union Ave via Santa Fe Ave and W 1st St.

GPS Coordinates: 38.2720° N, 104.6125° W

Nearest Town: Pueblo, CO

Interesting Facts: The museum sits on the original 1840s El Pueblo trading post site, connecting to the past.

SALIDA

Arkansas River

Why You Should Visit: The Arkansas River in Salida is a haven for outdoor adventure. Renowned for thrilling rapids and stunning scenery, it lures white-water rafters to feel the rush. Beyond rafting, fish, hike, bike, or picnic along the shores, reveling in Colorado's natural beauty.

Best Time to Visit: Late spring to early summer for snowmelt-fueled rapids. Fall brings quieter beauty with fall foliage.

Location: Salida, CO

Directions: From downtown Salida, head north on F St, turn right on W 1st St, left on G St, right on W Sackett Ave.

GPS Coordinates: 38.5347° N, 105.9989° W

Nearest Town: Salida, CO

Interesting Facts: Starting high in the Colorado mountains, the Arkansas is one of America's longest rivers, offering diverse recreation.

Monarch Mountain

Why You Should Visit: Monarch Mountain is a skier and snowboarder's treasure, offering exhilarating trails with less crowds than commercialized resorts. Catering to all levels with quality "champagne powder" snow, it's an authentic and unpretentious Rocky Mountain experience.

Best Time to Visit: The season runs late November to early April, with peak conditions December-February.

Location: Salida, CO

Directions: From Salida, take US-50 W about 20 minutes to the slopes.

GPS Coordinates: 38.5121° N, 106.3320° W

Nearest Town: Salida, CO

Interesting Facts: One of Colorado's oldest ski resorts, Monarch provides genuine skiing and riding without pretense.

Salida Hot Springs Aquatic Center

Why You Should Visit: Home to America's largest indoor hot springs, the Salida Hot Springs Aquatic Center promises relaxation and rejuvenation. With both lap and soaking pools, it caters to workouts or just peaceful unwinding. The contrast of warm waters and cool air makes winter visits especially serene.

Best Time to Visit: Open year-round, but winter and early spring are ideal.

Location: 410 W Rainbow Blvd, Salida, CO

Directions: From downtown Salida, head north on F St, turn right on W 3rd St, left on Holman Ave.

GPS Coordinates: 38.5430° N, 105.9972° W

Nearest Town: Salida, CO

Interesting Facts: The therapeutic mineral waters come from a local geothermal spring.

SILVERTON

Million Dollar Highway

(13)

Why You Should Visit: Stretching from Silverton to Ouray, the Million Dollar Highway stuns with twisting turns, dizzying heights, and breathtaking mountain vistas. This high-elevation route immerses you in Colorado's majesty, providing an otherworldly journey into the state's heart.

Best Time to Visit: Summer to early fall has clearer weather and less snow and ice.

Location: U.S. Highway 550 between Silverton and Ouray, CO

Directions: From Silverton, follow US-550 N to Ouray along the Million Dollar Highway.

GPS Coordinates: 37.8846° N, 107.7281° W

Nearest Town: Silverton, CO

Interesting Facts: Despite its beauty, the narrow, guardrail-less road is considered one of America's most dangerous drives, thrilling the daring.

Silverton Historical Jail

Why You Should Visit: Step into Silverton's intriguing past at the well-preserved Historical Jail. Old cells and artifacts provide a glimpse into the rugged lives of 19th/20th-century miners and settlers, while starkly showing how law and order operated in this remote mountain town.

Best Time to Visit: Summer, when weather is ideal and the town is lively.

Location: 1557 Greene St, Silverton, CO

Directions: From downtown Silverton, head north on Greene St. The jail is on the left.

GPS Coordinates: 37.8119° N, 107.6645° W

Nearest Town: Silverton, CO

Interesting Facts: Part of the larger San Juan County Historical Society preserving Silverton's heritage.

Molas Pass

Why You Should Visit: Molas Pass stuns with panoramic San Juan Mountain views and trails perfect for hiking and biking. Experience nature's grandeur through tranquil escapes or outdoor adventures along this scenic gateway.

Best Time to Visit: Summer through early fall when snow has melted, revealing lush landscapes and clear trails.

Location: U.S. Highway 550, Silverton, CO

Directions: From Silverton, head north on US-550 N for about 6.6 miles.

GPS Coordinates: 37.7425° N, 107.6889° W

Nearest Town: Silverton, CO

Interesting Facts: Part of the picturesque San Juan Skyway drive. It also lies on the 500+ mile Colorado Trail from Denver to Durango.

STEAMBOAT SPRINGS

Strawberry Park Hot Springs

Why You Should Visit: Nestled amongst Routt National Forest's aspen and pines, Strawberry Park Hot Springs is a natural oasis. Its mineral-rich waters provide tranquil relaxation against scenic mountain vistas for a quintessential Colorado experience.

Best Time to Visit: Winter is magical with surrounding snow, but summer/fall also allow warm soaks.

Location: 44200 Co Rd 36, Steamboat Springs, CO

Directions: From Steamboat Springs, head NW on Lincoln Ave, turn on 3rd St, left on Fish Creek Falls Rd, continue on Co Rd 36.

GPS Coordinates: 40.5013° N, 106.8702° W

Nearest Town: Steamboat Springs, CO

Interesting Facts: With rustic charm and minimal development, it offers a traditional hot springs mountain getaway.

Fish Creek Falls

Why You Should Visit: Fish Creek Falls is a remarkable Steamboat Springs spectacle, with waters roaring down a towering 283 feet. Surrounded by lush greenery or blanketed in snow, its beauty and power create an awe-inspiring natural wonder.

Best Time to Visit: Spring and early summer when snowmelt fuels the mighty cascade.

Location: Fish Creek Fall Rd, Steamboat Springs, CO

Directions: From downtown Steamboat, head north on Lincoln Ave, turn right on 3rd Street, left on Fish Creek Falls Road.

GPS Coordinates: 40.4902° N, 106.7561° W

Nearest Town: Steamboat Springs, CO

Interesting Facts: Seen on the Coors label, the easily accessible falls are popular with locals and visitors.

Steamboat Ski Resort

Why You Should Visit: Known as "Ski Town, U.S.A," Steamboat lures snow lovers with diverse trails for all levels amid friendly, small-town vibes. Beyond skiing and snowboarding, try snowmobiling, snowshoeing, or tubing in the area's picturesque setting.

Best Time to Visit: Peak winter months, December-February, have optimal snow conditions.

Location: 2305 Mt Werner Cir, Steamboat Springs, CO

Directions: From downtown Steamboat, head SE on Lincoln Ave, turn right on Walton Creek Rd, left on Mt Werner Rd.

GPS Coordinates: 40.4572° N, 106.8050° W

Nearest Town: Steamboat Springs, CO

Interesting Facts: Famed for its trademarked Champagne Powder® snow - light, dry, and fluffy!

Rabbit Ears Pass

Why You Should Visit: A mecca for outdoor adventure, Rabbit Ears Pass offers hiking, biking, and wildlife viewing in summer and snow sports in winter. The pass itself stuns with panoramic mountain and valley views.

Best Time to Visit: December-March for snow activities. June-August for summer sports.

Location: US-40, Steamboat Springs, CO

Directions: From Steamboat Springs, head SE on Lincoln Ave, continue on US-40 E through the pass.

GPS Coordinates: 40.3775° N, 106.5450° W

Nearest Town: Steamboat Springs, CO

Interesting Facts: Named after the nearby Rabbit Ears Peak, which resembles a pair of ears.

TELLURIDE

Telluride Ski Resort

Why You Should Visit: A crown jewel of Colorado skiing, Telluride lures snow-lovers with diverse trails amid stunning San Juan Mountain scenery. Renowned for challenging runs, family-friendly vibes, and pristine snow, it's a winter wonderland. After the slopes, enjoy charming Telluride town.

Best Time to Visit: Ski season runs late November to early April, with peak conditions December-February.

Location: 565 Mountain Village Blvd, Telluride, CO

Directions: From Telluride, take CO-145 S and Mountain Village Blvd.

GPS Coordinates: 37.9375° N, 107.8123° W

Nearest Town: Telluride, CO

Interesting Facts: With smaller crowds than other resorts, Telluride offers a more intimate and secluded ski experience.

Telluride Mountain Village Gondola

Why You Should Visit: More than transit, the Telluride Mountain Village Gondola offers a scenic ride with breathtaking San Juan Mountain views. Gliding over aspens and snow-capped peaks, this free public transportation is a serene experience.

Best Time to Visit: The gondola runs year-round; summer, fall, and winter showcase peak scenery.

Location: Stations at Telluride (Oak St), Mountain Village, San Sophia Overlook.

Directions: From downtown Telluride, head to the Oak Street station.

GPS Coordinates: 37.9376° N, 107.8126° W (Telluride station)

Nearest Town: Telluride, CO

Interesting Facts: This zero-emissions gondola has run on solar-supplemented electricity since 1996.

Bear Creek Falls

Why You Should Visit: Nestled in the San Juans, Bear Creek Falls is a hidden gem cascading picturesquely over rocky cliffs and lush greenery, attracting photographers and nature lovers. The serene trail to the falls passes wildflower meadows and forests.

Best Time to Visit: Late spring to early summer when snowmelt swells the falls and wildflowers bloom.

Location: Trailhead at the end of Pine St, Telluride

Directions: From downtown Telluride, head south on Pine St to the Bear Creek Trailhead.

GPS Coordinates: 37.9239° N, 107.8129° W

Nearest Town: Telluride, CO

Interesting Facts: The 2.5-mile hike (one way) provides a rewarding half-day adventure with gradual elevation gain.

Lizard Head Pass

Why You Should Visit: Lizard Head Pass rewards with dramatic San Juan Mountain views, including its namesake, the uniquely shaped Lizard Head Peak. The pass is the gateway to hiking, biking, and camping adventures, attracting outdoor enthusiasts. The scenic drive to the pass thrills with winding roads amid soaring peaks.

Best Time to Visit: Summer and early fall have ideal weather to explore the pass and trails without snow.

Location: On Highway 145 between Telluride and Dolores

Directions: From Telluride, head southwest on CO-145. The pass is 13 miles away.

GPS Coordinates: 37.8119° N, 108.1324° W

Nearest Town: Telluride, CO

Interesting Facts: Lizard Head Peak resembles a lizard's head and is one of Colorado's most challenging climbs.

VAIL

Vail Ski Resort

Why You Should Visit: Renowned for expansive terrain, modern amenities, and an alpine village ambiance, Vail lures winter enthusiasts with diverse slopes for all abilities. Its vibrant base village brims with charming shops, eateries, and lodging for a quintessential mountain resort experience.

Best Time to Visit: Visit December-March when blanketed in snow for a true winter wonderland.

Location: Vail, CO, nestled in the Rocky Mountains

Directions: From Denver, take I-70 W to exit 176 for Vail, follow signs to Vail Road.

GPS Coordinates: 39.6403° N, 106.3742° W

Nearest Town: Vail, CO

Interesting Facts: One of the world's largest resorts, Vail is famous for its sprawling 6-mile "Back Bowls."

Betty Ford Alpine Gardens

Why You Should Visit: America's highest botanical garden, Betty Ford Alpine Gardens is a high-altitude sanctuary displaying diverse mountain plants and delicate alpine blooms along winding paths. Educational exhibits illuminate nature's resilience and beauty.

Best Time to Visit: Summer from June-August sees peak blooms against the mountain backdrop.

Location: 522 S Frontage Rd E, Vail, CO

Directions: From Vail Resort, head east on Frontage Rd W, turn left on Vail Valley Dr. It's on the right.

GPS Coordinates: 39.6403° N, 106.3742° W

Nearest Town: Vail, CO

Interesting Facts: Named for former First Lady Betty Ford, a Vail resident and community contributor.

Gerald R. Ford Amphitheater

Why You Should Visit: The Gerald R. Ford Amphitheater is Vail's hub for cultural and musical events against a stunning mountain backdrop. With seating for over 2,500, it hosts concerts, ballets, movies, and more. Beyond the performances, soak in the natural beauty surrounding this scenic venue.

Best Time to Visit: The busy summer season from June to August brings lively programming.

Location: 530 S Frontage Rd E, Vail, CO

Directions: From Betty Ford Gardens, head SW on Frontage Rd W, right on Vail Valley Dr, right on E Meadow Dr.

GPS Coordinates: 39.6425° N, 106.3772° W

Nearest Town: Vail, CO

Interesting Facts: Named for President Gerald R. Ford, reflecting his and Betty Ford's deep Vail ties.

WINTER PARK

Winter Park Resort

Why You Should Visit: With over 3,000 acres of skiable terrain, Winter Park Resort is a haven for snowsports, tubing, snowcat tours, and more come winter. In summer, opt for mountain biking, hiking, zip lining and other warm weather adventures. It's an all-seasons hub for outdoor enthusiasts.

Best Time to Visit: November-April for snow sports. June-August for summer activities.

Location: 85 Parsenn Rd, Winter Park, CO

Directions: From Denver, take I-70 W and US-40 W to Winter Park. About a 90 minute drive.

GPS Coordinates: 39.8868° N, 105.7625° W

Nearest Town: Winter Park, CO

Interesting Facts: In operation since 1939, it's one of Colorado's oldest ski resorts.

Fraser Tubing Hill

Why You Should Visit: Fraser Tubing Hill offers classic snowy fun - zoom down groomed lanes on inner tubes, feeling the rush of mountain air. Safe for all ages, it's a way to relish winter's beauty even if you don't ski or snowboard.

Best Time to Visit: The prime tubing season is late November through early April.

Location: 455 Co Rd 72, Fraser, CO

Directions: From Winter Park, head north on US-40 E a short drive to Fraser.

GPS Coordinates: 39.9445° N, 105.8170° W

Nearest Town: Fraser, CO

Interesting Facts: Nicknamed the "Icebox of the Nation" for its cold temps, Fraser is ideal for snow sports like tubing.

Cozens Ranch Museum

Why You Should Visit: Step back in time at Cozens Ranch Museum, once a stagecoach stop and pioneer home. Exhibits spotlight local history - early ranching, skiing, and the lives of Fraser Valley settlers. Explore the grounds to experience the frontier past.

Best Time to Visit: Open year-round, though summer provides pleasant outdoor exploring.

Location: 77849 US-40, Granby, CO

Directions: Located off US Highway 40, a short drive from Winter Park.

GPS Coordinates: 39.9214° N, 105.7860° W

Nearest Town: Fraser, CO

Interesting Facts: The first ranch and stage stop in Fraser Valley, it offers rare insights into early pioneer life.

Colorado Adventure: 2 Magic Itineraries Proposals

(14)

Colorado Expedition: Rocky Mountain Rendezvous

From majestic mountain peaks to charming historic towns, dive into Colorado's wonders on a 7-day adventure showcasing the state's iconic eclectic culture, sweeping natural beauty, and one-of-a-kind outdoor thrills that characterize this remarkable western destination.

Day 1 - Denver Start

- **Morning**: Kickstart your expedition in Denver. Begin with a stroll down Larimer Square, absorbing the city's historical essence.
- **Afternoon**: Explore the diverse collections at the Denver Art Museum.
- **Evening**: Unwind at Denver Botanic Gardens before heading for a local dinner in town.

Day 2 - Boulder Bound

- **Morning**: Short drive to Boulder. Start with a visit to the Pearl Street Mall for some local shopping and brunch.
- **Afternoon**: Hike the trails at Boulder Flatirons.
- **Evening**: Relax at Chautauqua Park with a picnic dinner amidst panoramic mountain views.

Day 3 - Estes Park and Rocky Mountain National Park

- **Morning**: Drive to Estes Park, take the Estes Park Aerial Tramway for splendid views.
- **Afternoon**: Venture into Rocky Mountain National Park. Explore some accessible trails and capture breathtaking vistas.
- **Evening**: Settle in Estes Park, exploring its quaint downtown area.

Day 4 - Trail Ridge Road to Grand Lake

- **Morning**: Traverse the Trail Ridge Road, stopping at overlooks for photos.
- **Afternoon**: Arrive in Grand Lake, explore the town and maybe rent a boat or kayak on the lake.
- **Evening**: Enjoy a lakeside dinner in Grand Lake.

Day 5 - Winter Park Adventure

- **Morning**: Short drive to Winter Park. Explore Winter Park Resort, partaking in mountain biking or hiking.
- **Afternoon**: Chill out at Fraser Tubing Hill.
- **Evening**: Explore the local dining scene in Winter Park.

Day 6 - Through Berthoud Pass to Georgetown

- **Morning**: Drive through Berthoud Pass, stopping for photos.

- **Afternoon**: Arrive in Georgetown, ride the Georgetown Loop Railroad.
- **Evening**: Explore historic downtown Georgetown.

Day 7 - Back to Denver

- **Morning**: Leisurely morning in Georgetown.
- **Afternoon**: Return drive to Denver, maybe stop at Golden for a quick tour of Coors Brewery.
- **Evening**: Final dinner in Denver, reminiscing on the week's adventures before preparing for your journey home the next day.

Colorado Enchantment: Southern Splendors

Prepare for a another week of memorable adventures as we voyage south from lively Denver to uncover an array of cultural gems, glimpse into rich history, and marvel at stunning natural spectacles blanketing Colorado's southern territories, where you'll have the grand opportunity to experience firsthand the magnificent treasures this beautiful region of the Centennial State has in store.

Day 1 - Denver to Colorado Springs

- **Morning**: Set sail from Denver to Colorado Springs. First stop, Garden of the Gods for a majestic start.
- **Afternoon**: Ascend Pikes Peak for an adrenaline rush and breathtaking views.
- **Evening**: Settle into Colorado Springs, maybe explore downtown or relax at your lodging.

Day 2 - Manitou Springs and Cripple Creek

- **Morning**: Short drive to Manitou Springs, hike the Manitou Incline.

- **Afternoon**: Head to Cripple Creek, explore the historic town, maybe visit the Mollie Kathleen Gold Mine.
- **Evening**: Drive back to Manitou Springs, soak at SunWater Spa.

Day 3 - Canon City Adventure

- **Morning**: Drive to Canon City, a gateway to Royal Gorge Bridge and Park.
- **Afternoon**: Walk across Royal Gorge Bridge, then maybe a scenic train ride along the Arkansas River.
- **Evening**: Return to Colorado Springs for a tranquil evening.

Day 4 - Salida Sojourn

- **Morning**: Journey to Salida, wander along the Arkansas River.
- **Afternoon**: Explore Salida's historic downtown, maybe venture to nearby hot springs.
- **Evening**: Relax in Salida, enjoy a local meal.

Day 5 - Gunnison to Crested Butte

- **Morning**: Drive to Gunnison, visit Black Canyon of the Gunnison National Park.
- **Afternoon**: Continue to Crested Butte, a picturesque mountain town.
- **Evening**: Explore Crested Butte, absorb its rustic charm.

Day 6 - Through McClure Pass to Glenwood Springs

- **Morning**: Drive through scenic McClure Pass towards Glenwood Springs.
- **Afternoon**: Arrive in Glenwood Springs, relax at Glenwood Hot Springs Pool.

- **Evening**: Stroll through Glenwood Springs, maybe a late afternoon hike to Hanging Lake.

Day 7 - Back North to Denver

- **Morning**: Enjoy a leisurely morning in Glenwood Springs, maybe visit Glenwood Caverns Adventure Park.
- **Afternoon**: Drive back to Denver, through scenic I-70, stopping at Vail for a quick exploration.
- **Evening**: Arrive back in Denver, reminisce about the southern adventures over a hearty meal.

Travel

Journal Section

DATE OF VISIT: _____

NUMBER OF DAYS SPENT: _____

WEATHER CONDITIONS

WHAT I VISITED

WHAT I BOUGHT

WHERE I SLEPT

WHERE I EAT

WHO I MET

SECTION TO MARK THE SCORE FROM 0 TO 10

0	1	2	3	4	5	6	7	8	9	10

THE MOST BEAUTIFUL MEMORY

Travel

Journal Section

DATE OF VISIT: _____

NUMBER OF DAYS SPENT: _____

WEATHER CONDITIONS

WHAT I VISITED

WHAT I BOUGHT

WHERE I SLEPT

WHERE I EAT

WHO I MET

SECTION TO MARK THE SCORE FROM 0 TO 10

| 0 | 1 | 2 | 3 | 4 | 5 | 6 | 7 | 8 | 9 | 10 |

THE MOST BEAUTIFUL MEMORY

Travel

Journal Section

DATE OF VISIT: _____

NUMBER OF DAYS SPENT: _____

WEATHER CONDITIONS

WHAT I VISITED

WHAT I BOUGHT

WHERE I SLEPT

WHERE I EAT

WHO I MET

SECTION TO MARK THE SCORE FROM 0 TO 10

| 0 | 1 | 2 | 3 | 4 | 5 | 6 | 7 | 8 | 9 | 10 |

THE MOST BEAUTIFUL MEMORY

Travel

Journal Section

DATE OF VISIT: _____

NUMBER OF DAYS SPENT: _____

WEATHER CONDITIONS

WHAT I VISITED

WHAT I BOUGHT

WHERE I SLEPT

WHERE I EAT

WHO I MET

SECTION TO MARK THE SCORE FROM 0 TO 10

| 0 | 1 | 2 | 3 | 4 | 5 | 6 | 7 | 8 | 9 | 10 |

THE MOST BEAUTIFUL MEMORY

Travel

Journal Section

DATE OF VISIT: _____

NUMBER OF DAYS SPENT: _____

WEATHER CONDITIONS

WHAT I VISITED

WHAT I BOUGHT

WHERE I SLEPT

WHERE I EAT

WHO I MET

SECTION TO MARK THE SCORE FROM 0 TO 10

| 0 | 1 | 2 | 3 | 4 | 5 | 6 | 7 | 8 | 9 | 10 |

THE MOST BEAUTIFUL MEMORY

THE COLORADO TRAVELER LIFEJACKET BIBLE

Hassle-free Colorado Trip: Avoid These 11 Common Mistakes for a Smooth Colorado Vacation

Though an exploration of Colorado's majestic mountains, lush valleys, and winding trails promises adventure, avoiding common pitfalls can make your travels smoother and more rewarding. This helpful guide highlights 11 frequent mistakes made in the Centennial State's wild terrain, arming you with insider knowledge so you can deftly navigate its diverse landscapes and distinctive culture. Heed this advice so the wonders of Denver's vibrant streets, Boulder's lively college vibe, and the state's roaring rivers and scenic byways unlock only their richest, most unforgettable prizes for you on your upcoming voyage.

1. Underestimating Weather Variability

The skies over Colorado can shift from clear to stormy in a matter of minutes, especially during summer afternoons. Having a variety of layers on hand can save the day. A waterproof jacket is a smart choice to combat unexpected rain showers, while a hat and sunglasses will serve you well under the radiant mountain sun.

2. Overlooking Altitude Adjustments

The lofty heights of the Rockies can catch flatlanders off guard. Spend a day or two acclimating in Denver or Colorado Springs before heading to higher elevations. Stay hydrated and listen to your body. If you feel light-headed or unusually tired, take it easy and allow more time to adjust.

3. Ignoring Traction Laws

When winter descends, Colorado's roads can become icy and treacherous. The state enforces traction laws requiring snow tires or chains during adverse conditions. Heed the regulations to avoid hefty fines and keep the roads safe for everyone.

4. Skipping Advanced Reservations

Colorado's iconic destinations like Rocky Mountain National Park or the historic Strater Hotel in Durango fill up quickly, especially during peak seasons. Secure your lodging and any special tours or activities well in advance to ensure you don't miss out on the experiences atop your Colorado bucket list.

5. Not Checking Road Conditions

Whether due to sudden snowstorms or summer construction, road closures are a reality here. Stay updated on the latest conditions via local news outlets or the Colorado Department of Transportation's website to avoid unexpected detours that could derail your day.

6. Overdressing

Colorado attire leans towards the casual and functional. Swap the high heels and dress shoes for a comfortable pair of hiking boots or sneakers. You'll fit right in and be ready for whatever adventures come your way.

7. Disregarding Outdoor Etiquette

Coloradoans cherish their stunning natural surroundings. Adhere to leave-no-trace principles by packing out all trash, staying on designated trails, and respecting wildlife by keeping a safe distance. These simple actions contribute to the preservation of Colorado's wild beauty for generations to come.

8. Overlooking Off-Peak Seasons

The rush of summer and winter bring crowds to Colorado's most cherished spots. Consider a visit during the spring or fall shoulder seasons. You'll encounter fewer crowds, and the mild weather may offer a more relaxed and personal connection with the stunning landscapes.

9. Ignoring Local Laws, Especially Marijuana Laws

While recreational marijuana is legal in Colorado, public consumption is not. Be sure to familiarize yourself with the local laws regarding where you can purchase and consume marijuana to avoid any legal complications during your visit.

10. Misjudging Distance and Travel Times

Colorado's vast and diverse terrain can be deceptive when it comes to judging distances and travel times between destinations. What appears to be a short distance on a map can turn into a long, winding journey through mountainous roads. Ensure you allow ample time for travel, and be prepared for the journey to take longer than anticipated, especially if you're venturing into the high country or exploring scenic byways.

11. Neglecting Hydration

The dry climate, coupled with higher altitudes, can lead to dehydration faster than you might expect. It's crucial to drink plenty of water throughout the day to stay hydrated, even if you don't feel thirsty. This is especially important if you're engaging in physical activities like hiking or skiing. Carrying a reusable water bottle and refilling it frequently is a practical way to ensure you remain hydrated and energized to fully enjoy your Colorado adventure.

Did You Enjoyed Your Colorado Bucket List Guide Book?

Help fellow wanderers craft the perfect vacation by considering a review!

Penning down your experience is not only swift but pivotal in aiding travelers in selecting the ideal guide.

Your wisdom will steer them towards a dreamy holiday, bypassing the mundane and ensuring they grace all the must-see wonders. Your review can uplift someone else's vacation from good to unforgettable!

Navigate to the orders section of your Amazon profile and bestow your insights if this guide enriched your journey!

FREE DOWNLOAD!

Sign up for the **Telegramletter** list to receive free content and interesting updates,

and get right now a free copy of the Guide

"Colorado Season-by-Season 2023/2024"!

Scan the code below to join the **Telegramletter** and

download it for free!

Recommendation

Visit the link from your smartphone or laptop for a better experience.

Made in United States
Troutdale, OR
12/15/2023